BORA BORA TRAVEL GUIDE 2024

Discover the Attractions, Activities, and Accommodations for Your Dream Vacation in 2024

Luz F. Smith

Table of content

Introduction

Welcome to Bora Bora

Bora Bora is a small island in French Polynesia, located in the South Pacific Ocean. It is one of the most popular and picturesque places in the world, noted for its breathtaking lagoon, coral reefs, and overwater bungalows. Bora Bora is also a destination of rich culture, history, and adventure, where you may enjoy the warm hospitality of the Polynesian people, the interesting customs of their predecessors, and the exhilarating activities that nature offers. Whether you are searching for a romantic break, a family holiday, or a single experience, Bora Bora has something for everyone. In this guide, we will help you plan your vacation to Bora Bora, and give you some suggestions and recommendations on how to make the most of your stay.

Why Visit in 2024

Here are reasons why you should visit Bora Bora in 2024:

1. Bora Bora is one of the most beautiful islands in the world, with a dormant volcano at its core surrounded by a blue lagoon and coral reefs. You may enjoy spectacular views of the island from your overwater cottage, or explore the underwater wonders with snorkeling, diving, or swimming with sharks and rays.

2. Bora Bora provides a choice of activities for all tastes and budgets, from sunbathing on the white-sand beaches of Matira Beach to hiking up Mount Otemanu for panoramic views of the island. You can also enjoy the Polynesian culture and food with a traditional dance display, a canoe excursion, or a visit to a pearl farm.

3. Bora Bora is a fantastic spot for a romantic holiday, a honeymoon, or an anniversary celebration. You can pamper yourself and your loved one with a spa treatment, a candlelit supper, or a sunset cruise. You can

also make your trip more unique with a helicopter tour, a private island lunch, or a vow renewal ceremony.

4. Bora Bora is more accessible and affordable than ever, thanks to new aircraft routes, travel offers, and strategies to save money. You can fly directly to Bora Bora from Los Angeles, San Francisco, or Honolulu, or connect via Tahiti or Moorea. You can also get discounts on resorts, activities, and meals by reserving in advance, vacationing off-season, or joining a loyalty program.

If you are looking for a once-in-a-lifetime getaway to a tropical paradise, Bora Bora is the place to go in 2024. You will not regret it!

Geography of Bora Bora

Bora Bora is an island group in the Leeward Islands, which are part of the Society Islands of French Polynesia in the Pacific Ocean. The island group comprises the main island of Bora Bora and various smaller islands and atolls, such as Tūpai. The main island has a land area of

30.55 km 2 (12 sq mi) and is bordered by a lagoon and a barrier reef. The lagoon is home to rich marine life and is popular for snorkeling and diving. The main island features two extinct volcanic summits, Mount Pahia and Mount Otemanu, which rise to 658 m (2,159 ft) and 727 m (2,385 ft) respectively. The highest peak on the island is Mount Otemanu. The main hamlet and administrative hub of the island is Vaitape, which is located on the western side of the main island. The island has a tropical environment with moderate temperatures and heavy humidity throughout the year. The island is a significant tourist attraction, recognized for its luxury resorts and picturesque beauty.

History of Bora Bora

Bora Bora. Its name means "First Born" in Tahitian, and it was inhabited by Polynesian traders and colonists about the 3rd century. The island was originally observed by a European in 1722 by Dutch explorer Jakob Roggeveen, and later visited by Captain James Cook in 1770 with the help of a Tahitian navigator, Tupaia. Bora

Bora was an independent monarchy until 1888, when it was captured by France and became part of French Polynesia in 1957. During World War II, the island was an important location for the United States military, and the airfield built by the Americans is still in use today. Bora Bora is famed for its lagoon, coral reef, white sand beaches, and luxury resorts. It is a prominent tourist destination, attracting visitors from all over the world who wish to experience its natural beauty and culture.

Chapter 1

Travel Essentials

Visa Requirements and Entry

If you plan to visit this tropical paradise, you may be wondering if you need a visa and what other entry conditions you must follow. This guide will provide you with all the information you need to know before visiting Bora Bora.

Do you need a visa to visit Bora Bora?

The answer is dependent on your nationality, the purpose and duration of your stay, and whether you want to visit other countries in the region. In general, travelers to Bora Bora do not require a visa for 90 days every six months. A passport must be valid for at least three months, and documentation of further travel may be necessary. No visas are necessary for US Americans, Canadians, Japanese, and New Zealanders visiting Bora Bora for more than one month. A passport valid for six months beyond the date of departure from French Polynesia is necessary.

However, some exclusions and unique conditions apply to specific nationalities and situations. For example, if you are a European Union citizen, you can stay in Bora Bora for up to 90 days without a visa, but you will need a visa if you wish to work, study, or stay longer than 90 days. If you are an Australian citizen, you can stay in Bora Bora for up to three months without a visa, but you will need a visa if you wish to work or study. If you are a citizen of a country that is not on the visa exemption list, you must apply for a visa before visiting Bora Bora.

To find out if you require a visa for Bora Bora, go to Frances official visa page. You can also inquire at the nearest French embassy or consulate in your place of residence about the exact visa requirements and application process for your case. It is best to apply for your visa well in advance of your trip date, as processing times vary based on the embassy or consulate.

What are the other entry requirements for Bora Bora?

Aside from having a valid passport and visa (if applicable), you must also complete several other entrance requirements to visit Bora Bora.

1. Proof of a return or onward ticket: You must show that you have a confirmed ticket to leave French Polynesia before your visa-free period or visa ends. This is to keep you from overstaying and becoming an illegal immigrant.

2. Evidence of sufficient funds: You must demonstrate that you have enough money to pay your expenses in Bora Bora, such as lodging, food, and transportation. This is to guarantee that you do not become a burden to the local authorities or citizens. The amount of money required will vary based on the length and purpose of your vacation, but it is typically recommended that you have at least $50 per day accessible.

3. Proof of health insurance: You must have health insurance that covers medical expenses in the event of illness or accident while in Bora Bora. This is to safeguard you from having to pay exorbitant medical fees or being denied treatment. You can buy travel insurance coverage that includes French Polynesia before you go, or you can see if your current health insurance covers you abroad.

4. Proof of COVID-19 vaccine or negative test: Due to the continuing COVID-19 pandemic, you must present proof of immunization or a negative PCR test done within 72 hours of your departure to Bora Bora. You must also complete an online health declaration form and acquire a QR code, which you will give upon arriving. During your stay, you may be subjected to random testing and health screening. More information regarding the COVID-19 travel restrictions and requirements for

Bora Bora can be found on the official website of Tahiti Tourism.

Currency and Exchange

What currency does Bora Bora use?

The French Pacific Franc (XPF) is the local currency in Bora Bora. CFP is another name for the code. The currencies XPF and CFP are the same. As a result of its peg to the Euro, the XPF is a stable currency. Exchange rates fluctuate daily, although, in recent years, one US dollar has varied between 95 and 115 XPF.

What is the best way to exchange money in Bora Bora?

Depending on your desire and convenience, there are various ways to exchange money in Bora Bora. **Here are some of the most popular alternatives:**

1. ATMs: ATMs are available in most towns and resorts on Bora Bora, and they frequently offer better exchange rates than money changers. To prevent several ATM fees, withdraw larger sums of money at once and confirm that your card will be accepted on the island with your bank or credit card provider5. You can also withdraw funds in US dollars from some Tahitian banks.

2. Banks: The main island of Bora Bora has two banks: Banque Socredo and Banque de Polynésie. They are both in the main town of Vaitape. They provide currency exchange, money transfers, and traveler's checks. They are open from 8 a.m. to 3 p.m. Monday through Friday and from 8 a.m. to 11 a.m. on Saturday.

3. Currency exchange: There are two foreign exchange offices at Tahiti's Faa'a International Airport, where you will most likely arrive before boarding a domestic trip to Bora Bora. They are called Banque Socredo and Banque de Tahiti, and they are open every day from 6am to 9pm. If you want to visit Papeete, Tahiti's capital, before or after your trip to Bora Bora, you can also locate various money changers. Money changers, on the other hand, typically charge greater fees and give lower interest rates than ATMs or banks.

4. Credit cards: Credit cards are generally accepted in Bora Bora, particularly in hotels, restaurants, and retail establishments. The most common credit cards are Visa and MasterCard, however, certain establishments may also accept American Express or Diners Club. Credit cards are easy and safe, but your bank or card issuer may charge foreign transaction or currency conversion fees. To avoid these fees, select a travel-friendly credit card with no foreign transaction fees. You can also send and receive money online by using online payment services such as PayPal or TransferWise.

How much money should you bring with you to Bora Bora?

Based on firsthand experience, I'd suggest carrying only $100 to $200 in cash to Bora Bora. When you arrive in Tahiti, swap it for XPF at Faa'a Airport (PPT). Bora Bora doesn't require much cash because most places take credit cards. However, having some cash on hand for tips, souvenirs, and little purchases is usually a smart idea. You can also use cash to pay for activities such as snorkeling, diving, or boat tours, as some operators may give cash discounts.

What currencies should I bring to Bora Bora?

The XPF is the finest currency to take to Bora Bora because it is the island's official and most widely used currency. If you don't have access to XPF before your trip, you can bring US dollars, Euros, or Australian dollars, as these are the most easily exchanged currencies in Tahiti and Bora Bora. You can convert these currencies at the airport, banks, or money changers, but keep in mind the costs and rates. Alternatively, if your credit card or ATM card is compatible with the local machines and networks, you can use it to obtain XPF or USD on the island.

How does the US economy's strength affect the USD/Bora Bora exchange rate?

A robust US economy may cause the dollar to strengthen, resulting in a weaker USD/Bora Bora exchange rate. This implies you'll get less XPF for your USD, which could make your trip more expensive. A weaker US economy, on the other hand, may result in a weaker dollar, which may result in a greater USD/Bora Bora exchange rate.

Language Spoken

Tahitian is the language spoken in Bora Bora, and it is part of the Polynesian branch of the Austronesian language family. Tahitian is connected to other Polynesian languages such as Hawaiian, Maori, and Samoan. Tahitian is the national language of French Polynesia, which encompasses the islands of Tahiti, Moorea, Bora Bora, and Raiatea. Tahitian is also spoken in the Cook Islands, New Caledonia, and Niue.

Tahitian has a long and varied history that has been affected by numerous cultures and events. Bora Bora's original settlers arrived during the third century CE, bringing their ancient Polynesian language with them. The island was first seen by European explorers in 1722 when Dutch navigator Jakob Roggeveen visited it. Later, in 1769, British explorer James Cook arrived with a Tahitian navigator named Tupaia, who assisted him in communicating with the islanders. Bora Bora, along with the other Society Islands, became a French colony in 1842. Since then, French has been the official language of administration, education, and business, while Tahitian has remained the language of everyday life and culture.

Tahitian is a fascinating language with many distinct traits and idioms. Tahitian has only 16 letters in its alphabet: five vowels (a, e, i, o, u) and 11 consonants (f, h, k, m, n, p, r, t, v, x, z). Tahitian can not discriminate between the sounds [p] and [b], or between [t] and [d], hence the sound represented by p falls between the two, as does t. Tahitian also contains a sound comparable to [l] and [r], represented by r. Bora Bora, for example, is pronounced [poa poa] in Tahitian.

Tahitian is an expressive and poetic language, with numerous words and phrases reflecting the island's culture and surroundings. Tahitian has various words for different shades of blue, such as Moana (ocean blue), tr (sky blue), and pai (deep blue). Tahitian has various words for different forms of rain, including ua roa (long rain), ua tree (sudden rain), and ua rere (flying rain). Tahitian has several idioms and proverbs, such as "E tahi te fa'a'ari'ara'a, e tahi te fa'aso'o" (One is the method of doing, one is the way of being happy), which means that everyone has their style of living and being happy.

Tahitian is a living and growing language, reacting to the modern world and the influences of other languages. Tahitian has adopted many words from French, including farni (French), pere' (bicycle), and tv (television). Tahitian has also developed new words from existing ones, such as 'pita (hospital), from 'pi (ill) and ta'ata (person), or 'rara'a (radio), from 'ra (sound) and ra'a (sun).. Tahitian has also learned English, particularly in the tourism business, where many visitors are from English-speaking nations. Tahitian can greet English speakers with "Ia ora na" (Hello) or "Murumuru" (Thank you).

Tahitian is a language worth knowing and respecting since it displays the beauty and diversity of Bora Bora and its people. Tahitian is a basic language with phonetic spelling and simple grammar. Tahitian is a wonderful language to learn since it has a musical and rhythmic tone. Tahitian is a rich and sophisticated language with a long and varied history as well as a vibrant and innovative culture. Tahitian is the language of Bora Bora, and you will adore it.

Chapter 2

Best Time to Visit

Weather Overview

Bora Bora's weather is warm and humid all year, with temperatures ranging from 25°C to 30°C on average. There are, however, two different seasons: rainy and dry. November to April is the wet season, and May to October is the dry season.

Rain showers, high humidity, and gloomy skies characterize the rainy season. This season's average rainfall is around 180 mm per month, while the average humidity is at 80%. The wet season is also the cyclone season, thus high winds and storms are possible. Cyclones, on the other hand, are uncommon in Bora Bora, and the majority of the rain falls in brief spurts, leaving plenty of sunny periods.

Bora Bora is most popular during the dry season since it has more sunshine, less rain, and lower humidity. This season's average rainfall is around 70 mm per month, while the average humidity is at 70%. The dry season is also the peak tourist season, which means higher prices, more crowds, and less availability. Outdoor activities including snorkeling, diving, hiking, and sailing are great during the dry season.

Bora Bora's best time to visit varies on your interests, money, and activities. If you don't mind rain and prefer to avoid crowds, the wet season may be a suitable choice for you. Lower rates, bigger discounts, and greater flexibility are also available. If you enjoy bright, dry weather and are willing to pay a higher price, the dry season may be a better option for you. In addition, you can enjoy the highest visibility, water temperature, and marine life.

Peak Tourist Seasons

Prices and Crowds

Bora Bora is a renowned tourist destination, drawing visitors from all over the world. The peak tourist seasons on the island are June to August and December to January. This means that resorts, restaurants, and tours will be more crowded and costlier. If you want to avoid crowds and save money, go during the low or shoulder seasons. The low season, which coincides with the wet season, lasts from December to March. The shoulder seasons, which are the transition months between the dry and wet seasons, are April and November. You can discover reduced rates on accommodations and flights during certain times, as well as more space and privacy on the island.

Festivals and events

Bora Bora has a dynamic culture that has been impacted by its Polynesian roots as well as French colonization. Various events and festivals are held throughout the year to commemorate the island's history, traditions, and arts.

1. Tahiti Pearl Regatta (May): A sailing tournament held in the Leeward Islands, which includes Bora Bora. Sailors from all around the world engage in a variety of races and challenges. There are also cultural performances, concerts, and celebrations.

2. Heiva I Bora Bora (July): A cultural festival highlighting the island's music, dancing, and crafts. It includes classic and modern art competitions, performances, and exhibitions. It is an excellent opportunity to experience the island's vibrant culture.

3. Hawaiki Nui Va'a (November): This is a three-day canoe race around the islands of Huahine, Raiatea, Taha'a, and Bora Bora. It is one of Polynesia's most prestigious and difficult competitions, with hundreds of paddlers and thousands of spectators.

4. Bora Bora Liquid Festival (December): This is a water sports festival that celebrates the aquatic environment of the island. Swimming, stand-up paddle boarding, surfing, and kite surfing are among the activities offered. Music, yoga, and wellness events are also included.

Chapter 3

Getting There

Flights to Bora Bora

Getting to Bora Bora can be difficult because there are no direct flights from most major cities throughout the world. The only way to get to Bora Bora is to fly to Tahiti first, then take a domestic flight or a boat to the smaller island. **Here are tips and options for finding the best flights to Bora Bora.**

1. The main airport in Tahiti is Faa'a International Airport (PPT), which is about 5 kilometers from the capital city of Papeete. This is where you will arrive from your international flight and where you will connect your aircraft to Bora Bora. Air France, Air Tahiti Nui, Air New Zealand, Hawaiian Airlines, United Airlines, and Qantas all fly to Tahiti from various locations. You may compare the pricing and schedules of

various airlines using online platforms like Expedia, Google Flights, Flight Centre, Skyscanner, and others.

2. The only airport in Bora Bora is Motu Mute Airport (BOB), which is located on a small islet north of the main island. Air Tahiti, French Polynesia's domestic carrier, is the only airline that flies to Bora Bora. Air Tahiti operates several flights every day from Tahiti to Bora Bora, with a journey time of about 50 minutes. Rates vary according to the season and demand, but a one-way ticket should cost between $200 and $300. You can book your flights to Bora Bora directly on the Air Tahiti website, or through a travel agent or a third-party website. However, keep in mind that certain websites may not show the availability of all flights, so be sure to check the Air Tahiti website as well.

3. Another way to get to Bora Bora from Tahiti is to take a boat or ferry. This is a less expensive and more scenic mode of transportation, but it takes longer and is not always available. Two main companies provide boat transportation to Bora Bora: Maupiti Express and Bora

Bora Cruises. Maupiti Express operates a fast catamaran that can take you to Bora Bora in around 3 hours, with a layover in Maupiti island. A one-way ticket costs around $100. Bora Bora Cruises provides a magnificent yacht that can transport you to Bora Bora in around 5 hours, with a stopover in Raiatea island. A one-way trip costs around $300. You can purchase boat tickets online or through a travel agent. However, keep in mind that these services are not available every day and are subject to weather and availability. As a result, it is recommended that you book ahead of time and confirm your departure and arrival times.

Transportation on the Island

By Bike

One of the greatest methods to move around Bora Bora is by bike, especially given that the entire island can be covered in a few hours. Another option is to rent a car, which is substantially more expensive than renting a bicycle. The main roads in and around Bora Bora are paved and in good shape, and you may ride around while admiring the scenery of the lagoon, mountains, and palm palms. You can also visit Matira Beach, Bloody Mary's restaurant, and the Marae Aehautai (an ancient temple site). Bike rental companies like Europcar and Avis rent bikes for approximately $20 per day, and there are a couple of bike-rental kiosks along Matira Beach. Your resort may also hire bikes.

By Car, Scooter, or Motorcycle

To move around Bora Bora with more freedom and speed, you can rent a vehicle, scooter, or motorbike. This option, however, is more expensive and necessitates the possession of a valid driver's license. Cars can be rented at the airport or various Bora Bora resorts (including the InterContinental Bora Bora Le Moana Resort and the Sofitel Bora Bora Marara Beach Resort). Some places even rent bikes, scooters, and buggies. A car should cost roughly $100 per day, a scooter $50, and a motorcycle $70. You can also schedule a guided tour in conjunction with a 4x4 safari to explore the island's rocky interior and have a unique trip.

By Boat

Another option for getting around Bora Bora is via boat, which is required if you choose to stay on one of the tiny motu (islets) that encircle the main island. Most resorts provide airport transfers and island shuttles via boat, either for free or for a fee, depending on the property. Private transfer boats, such as Dino's Land & Water Taxi or Taxi Motu, may carry you anywhere in the lagoon for around $25. Boating is also a fantastic way to enjoy the Bora Bora's popular water sports, such as snorkeling, diving, fishing, and sailing. You can take a boat excursion to the lagoon's top places, such as the coral gardens, shark and ray feeding, and sunset cruise.

By Bus or a Taxi

Bora Bora's only public transportation is Le Truck, a bus that runs every hour or so around the island and back. However, owing to COVID-19, this service is unreliable and may not be available. Taxis are also available, but they are highly expensive; depending on the time of day, a ride from Vaitape (the main town) to the Matira Point hotel district may cost between $15 and $20. As a result, unless you have no other options, these are not suggested.

By foot

Finally, you can explore Bora Bora on foot, which is an excellent opportunity to learn about the local culture and wildlife. You can walk down the 18-mile-long seaside route, stopping in little villages, shops, and marketplaces along the way. Hike to Mount Otemanu, the island's highest summit, for breathtaking views of the lagoon and surrounding islands. However, you should be warned that the trip is difficult and requires a guide due to the lack of documented pathways and the steep and rocky terrain.

As you can see, depending on your budget, preference, and itinerary, there are numerous ways to move around Bora Bora. You will undoubtedly appreciate the beauty and diversity of this island paradise whether you prefer to cycle, cruise, or walk.

Car Rentals

You may explore this paradise on your own by renting a car and driving around the island. **Here are eight automobile rental alternatives in Bora Bora to think about:**

1. Avis Bora Bora: This is the island's leading automobile rental firm, as well as the first to rent electric vehicles in French Polynesia. They provide a wide range of vehicles, including cars, electric fun cars, mopeds, and motorcycles. You can pick up and drop off your vehicle from anywhere on the island, and you can use their free app (Bora Bora Explorer) to get your recommendations and suggestions. They have 4.5-star ratings on Google, Facebook, and Tripadvisor, as well as several good client reviews.

2. Expedia: A prominent online travel service that allows you to compare and reserve vehicle rentals in Bora Bora from several vendors. You can also save money by bundling your car rental with a flight or hotel stay, and most car rentals allow for penalty-free cancellation. You can select an economy, compact, midsize, or SUV car and pay in person or online.

3. Rentcars: A global car rental platform that connects you to the top car rental providers in Bora Bora and other destinations. You can search for, compare, and reserve a car online, paying in your native currency or with a credit card. You can also cancel or alter your reservation for free and get customer service 24 hours a day, seven days a week.

4. Booking.com: Another well-known online travel operator that provides low-cost vehicle rentals in Bora Bora and other locations. You may search for and reserve a car from the world's largest brands, with flexible cancellation policies and no hidden fees. On their website and app, you may also get excellent offers on hotels, flights, and activities.

5. Europcar: Europcar is a multinational vehicle rental firm that has a branch in Bora Bora near the Vaitape dock. They provide automobiles ranging from affordable to luxury, as well as electric cars and scooters. You can book online or over the phone, and you can cancel or change your reservation for free up to 48 hours before pickup. In addition, they offer a complimentary shuttle service from the airport or your hotel to their office.

6. Bora Bora Fun Car: This is a local car rental company that specializes in electric fun cars, which are compact, open-air vehicles that can seat up to four people. They're excellent for touring the island at your leisure while taking in the scenery and breeze. You can rent them by the hour, half-day, or full-day, and they can be delivered and picked up from your hotel or any other spot on the island. They also supply a map and a guidebook with tour suggestions.

7. Bora Bora Scooters: Another local car rental firm that rents out scooters and bikes. They feature models ranging from classic to sporty, as well as electric motorcycles. You can rent them by the hour, day, or week, with helmets, locks, and insurance included. In Vaitape, you can also buy souvenirs, food, and drinks.

8. Bora Bora Rent a Car: This is a family-owned and operated car rental company that has been in business since 1992. They have a car, van, and truck fleet as well as electric cars and scooters. You can rent a car by the day or by the week, and they will bring and pick up the car from your hotel or any other point on the island. Long-term rentals and group bookings are also discounted.

Chapter 4

Accommodation

Hostel

Bora Bora's Top 5 Luxury Budget Hostels

1. InterContinental Bora Bora Resort Thalasso Spa, an IHG Hotel: This is one of the most opulent resorts in Bora Bora, featuring huge and exquisite overwater villas overlooking the lagoon and Mount Otemanu. A spa, a fitness center, a pool, a restaurant, and a bar are also available at the resort. Snorkeling, kayaking, paddle boarding, and diving are all options. The resort is located on a private motu (islet), so you'll need to take a boat from the airport or the main island to get there. A night at an overwater villa costs $1,200, but there are some specials and reductions available if you book ahead of time or during low season.

2. Sofitel Bora Bora Private Island: This is another premium resort on a secluded motu with overwater bungalows and beach villas. A private beach, a restaurant, a bar, a library, and a solarium are all available at the resort. You can also use the neighboring Sofitel Bora Bora Marara Beach Resort's facilities and services, which include a pool, spa, and water sports center. The resort offers complimentary boat transfers to and from the main island, as well as snorkeling and kayaking equipment. A night in an overwater cottage costs $900, but their website also has some special discounts and bundles.

3. Bora Bora Pearl Beach Resort & Spa: A four-star resort includes overwater bungalows, beach suites, and garden villas with private pools. The spa, fitness center, pool, tennis court, restaurant, and bar are all available at the resort. Snorkeling, kayaking, canoeing, jet skiing, and parasailing are all options. The resort is on a motu facing the main island, and you will need to take a boat from the airport or the main island to get there. A night in an overwater cottage costs $800, however, there are occasional promos and deals available on their website.

4. Hotel Le Meridien Bora Bora: A four-star resort boasting overwater bungalows and beach villas with direct lagoon access. A spa, a fitness center, a pool, two restaurants, and a bar are available at the resort. Snorkeling, kayaking, paddle boarding, and sailing are all options. The resort is on a motu near the main island, and you will need to take a boat from the airport or the main island to get there. A night in an overwater house costs $700, but discounts and bundles are available on their website.

5. Polynesia, Maitai Bora Bora: On the main island of Bora Bora, this three-star hotel provides overwater bungalows and garden rooms. A private beach, a restaurant, a bar, and a souvenir shop are all available at the hotel. You can go snorkeling, kayaking, biking, or hiking. The hotel is situated on the island's south-eastern shore, close to Matira Beach and Point Matira. A night in an overwater cottage costs $500, but their website also has some discounted rates and discounts.

Bora Bora Low-Cost Hostels

1. Bora Bora Eco Lodge: This is a budget-friendly guesthouse on the main island of Bora Bora that provides bungalows and dorm rooms. A communal kitchen, a lounge, a terrace, and a garden are available at the guesthouse. You may go snorkeling, kayaking, fishing, and cycling. The guesthouse sits on the island's northwestern shore, close to Vaitape and the airport. A night in a bungalow costs $150, while a night in a dorm room is $50.

2. Sunset Hill Lodge: This is a low-cost guesthouse on Bora Bora's main island that provides apartments and studios. There is a communal kitchen, a BBQ area, a washing room, and a car rental service at the guesthouse. You can go snorkeling, kayaking, diving, or sailing. The guesthouse sits on the island's northwestern shore, near Vaitape and the airport. A night in an apartment starts at $120, and a night in a studio starts at $80.

3. Bora Bora Holiday's Lodge and Villa: This is a low-cost guesthouse on the main island of Bora Bora with villas and rooms. There is a common kitchen, a dining area, a lounge, and a garden at the guesthouse. You can go snorkeling, kayaking, hiking, or riding. The guesthouse is situated on the island's southwestern shore, close to Matira Beach and Point Matira. A night in a villa starts at $100, while a night in a room starts at $60.

4. Village Temanuata: This is a low-cost guesthouse on the main island of Bora Bora that offers bungalows and rooms. A private beach, a restaurant, a bar, and a water sports center are all available at the guesthouse. Activities such as snorkeling, kayaking, canoeing, and jet skiing are available. The guesthouse is situated on the island's south-eastern shore, close to Matira Beach and Point Matira. A night in a bungalow starts at $90, and a night in a room starts at $50.

5. Fare ARIITEA: This is a low-cost holiday home on Bora Bora's main island that offers a two-bedroom property with air conditioning. There is a kitchen, a washing machine, a flat-screen TV, and a patio in the vacation house. You may go snorkeling, kayaking, fishing, and cycling. The vacation property is located on the island's south-eastern shore, close to Matira Beach and Point Matira. A night at the residence costs $80.

Hotels

Bora Bora High Budget Hotel

1. Le Bora Bora by Pearl Resorts: This resort combines exquisite position with proximity to the mainland, as it is only a ten-minute boat trip from the airport and fifteen minutes across the lagoon from Vaitape. The resort has classic Polynesian style and architecture, as well as some of the most traditionally constructed rooms and villas on the island. Overwater bungalows, garden villas with pools, and beach villas with pools are available, all with spectacular views of Mount Otemanu. In addition, the resort boasts three restaurants, one bar, and a spa that offers sumptuous treatments made with local products. The average nightly price is $1,200.

2. Four Seasons Resort Bora Bora: A tropical paradise surrounded by turquoise oceans, white sand beaches, and lush flora, this resort is a must-see. The resort has 107 overwater bungalow suites and seven beachfront villa estates with traditional thatched roofs and Polynesian art decor. You may gaze out of your private plunge pool at the lagoon or the mountains, or you can take advantage of the resort's services, which include four restaurants, two bars, a spa, a fitness center, a tennis field, a kids club, and a water sports center. The average nightly fee is $1,500.

3. The St. Regis Bora Bora Resort: A dream come true, this resort has the largest overwater villas in the South Pacific, some with private pools, whirlpools, or outdoor showers. The Royal Estate, a 13,000-square-foot estate with three bedrooms, a private chef, a butler, and a spa, is also available at the resort. The resort includes five restaurants, including Jean-Georges' iconic Lagoon

Restaurant, which offers gourmet dining overlooking the water. There are two bars, a spa, a fitness facility, a kids club, and a private lagoonarium filled with tropical fish and coral. The average nightly rate is $2,000.00.

Bora Bora Low Cost Hotel

1. Royal Bora Bora: This hotel is a fantastic choice for those looking to experience the splendor of Bora Bora on a budget. The hotel has 80 rooms, each with a flat-screen TV, a refrigerator, and a minibar. There is also free wifi, parking, a pool, a poolside bar, and a coffee shop at the hotel. The hotel is strategically positioned near some of Bora Bora's greatest seafood restaurants, including Bloody Mary's, Matira Beach Restaurant, and Jean-Georges Lagoon Restaurant. The hotel is also near some of Bora Bora's most popular attractions, including Leopard Rays Trench, a coral where you can snorkel with beautiful creatures. The average nightly fee is $300.

2. Bora Bora Vaite Lodge: This beachfront holiday home provides guests with sustainable and environmentally friendly accommodations as well as spectacular sea views. The lodge is designed with natural materials and local art and features two bedrooms, a living area, a kitchen, a bathroom, and a patio. The resort also includes free wifi, shuttle service, private parking, and a playground for children. The lodge is located in a quiet and serene setting where you can listen to the waves and feel the breeze. The lodge is also close to a grocery store, and the lagoon and marina are only a few minutes away. The average nightly price is $200.

3. Bora Red Hibiscus Lodge: This attractive and comfortable Bora Bora lodging is located 2.8 kilometers from Matira Beach and 16 kilometers from Mount Otemanu. There is one bedroom, a living room, a kitchen, a bathroom, and a garden at the lodge. Air conditioning, free wifi, free parking, and a terrace are also available at the lodge. The lodge is non-smoking and located in a secure and private setting. The lodge is close to some of Bora Bora's greatest restaurants and shops, including Sibani Perles, a pearl boutique where you may purchase unusual and wonderful jewelry. The average nightly fee is $150.

4. Bora Rent Lodge: Located in Bora Bora, 3.9 kilometers from Mount Otemanu, this lodge is comfortable and convenient. The lodge consists of one bedroom, one living area, one kitchen, one bathroom, and one balcony. There is also air conditioning, free WiFi, free parking, and a bar at the resort. The lodge is non-smoking and conveniently located near the main sights and activities in Bora Bora, such as Reef Discovery Bora Bora, a tour business that offers snorkeling and diving expeditions in the lagoon. The average nightly price is $180.

5. Fare Luna - Comfy New property in Bora Bora: This property is a newly refurbished and large Bora Bora accommodation that provides guests with an environmentally friendly and modern stay. There are two bedrooms, a living room, a kitchen, a bathroom, and a yard in this house. There is also air conditioning, free wifi, free parking, and a terrace at the property. The house is non-smoking and nestled in a lovely tropical garden with views of the mountains and flowers. The residence is also close to some of Bora Bora's top beaches and lagoons, including Maitai Polynesia Bora Bora Beach, a white sand beach where you may swim, sunbathe, or kayak. The average nightly price is $230.

Camping

Camping is an inexpensive way to enjoy Bora Bora's natural beauty and culture. **Here are five camping choices for Bora Bora.**

1. Bora Eco Camping

Bora Éco Camping is a little motu (islet) on the main island of Bora Bora. It provides six rooms with minimal facilities like solar power, a communal shower, and a kitchen. Free activities include snorkeling, cultural exploration, and a coconut show. The campground also serves healthy vegetarian meals with the addition of fish, eggs, and cheese on occasion. Bora Éco Camping is suitable for those who want to experience nature while learning about Polynesian culture. A room can be booked for 30€ per night.

2. Bora Bora Backpacker Accommodation

Bora Bora Shelter For Backpackers is another camping option on Bora Bora's main island, near Matira Beach. Six rooms are available, each with a nice bed, a fan, and a mosquito net. You can also use the communal bathroom, kitchen, and lounge. The campground is adjacent to stores, restaurants, and activities including bike rentals, jet ski rides, and parasailing. Bora Bora Shelter For Backpackers is ideal for backpackers who wish to explore the island and meet other tourists. A room can be booked for 36€ per night.

3. Matira Camping Matira

Camping Matira is located near Matira Beach on the south end of the main island of Bora Bora. It rents out tents that include mattresses, pillows, and linens. You can also make use of the shared restroom, kitchen, and grill. The camping area is bordered by coconut palms and tropical flora, and it provides immediate beach access. You can also gaze out at the lagoon and watch the sunset. Camping Matira is ideal for visitors who want to experience beach life while relaxing in a calm setting. A tent can be rented for 25€ per night.

4. Richard's Campground

Camping Chez Richard is located on the east side of Bora Bora's main island, near Vaitape village. Bungalows with individual bathrooms, kitchens, and terraces are available. You may also take advantage of the garden, swimming pool, and complimentary Wi-Fi. The campground is near a store, a bank, and a ferry terminal. To explore the island, you can also rent a car, a bike, or a scooter. Camping Chez Richard is ideal for budget-conscious guests who desire more comfort and convenience. A bungalow can be rented for 50€ per night.

5. Bora Bora Camping

Camping Bora Bora is a camping area located on a secluded motu opposite Bora Bora's main island. It provides typical Polynesian bungalows with their bathroom, kitchen, and patio. The private beach, kayaks, and snorkeling equipment are also available. The campground also offers free shuttle service to and from the airport and the main island. Breakfast, lunch, and dinner are also available, using local and organic ingredients. Camping Bora Bora is suitable for guests seeking more solitude and exclusivity while remaining budget-conscious. A bungalow can be rented for 75€ per night.

Tips for booking Accommodation

1. Compare Bora Bora hotel prices from several websites. You can compare the rates, reviews, facilities, and locations of numerous hotels in Bora Bora by using a website like [KAYAK]. You can also search for hotels based on their kind, such as overwater bungalows, beachfront villas, or low-cost guesthouses. You might come across some exclusive bargains or discounts.

2. Consider staying on a motu or the main island. Bora Bora consists of a large island and a ring of motus, or smaller islets. The majority of the luxury resorts are located on the Motus, which provides spectacular views

of the lagoon and Mount Otemanu, but they are also more isolated and pricey. Staying on the main island gives you easier access to the town, stores, restaurants, and activities, as well as more affordable transportation alternatives. Some hotels on the main island, such as (InterContinental Bora Bora Thalasso Spa, an IHG Hotel), provide overwater bungalows with lagoon views.

3. Plan ahead of time for flights and hotel transfers; Bora Bora is difficult to get because you must first fly to Tahiti and then take a domestic flight to Bora Bora Airport, which is located on a motu. You must then take a boat shuttle to your hotel, which might cost between $50 and $200 per person, depending on the distance and the hotel. You should book your flights and hotel transfers in advance, preferably as a package offer, to minimize stress and save money. Check to see if your hotel has free or reduced airport transportation as part of your reservation.

4. Before booking, check the hotel policies and amenities: Bora Bora is an expensive resort, so you want

to make sure you receive the most bang for your buck. Check the hotel policies and facilities before booking, such as the cancellation policy, check-in and check-out timings, breakfast selections, Wi-Fi availability, resort fees, taxes, and tipping etiquette. Check to see whether any activities or amenities, such as snorkeling equipment, kayaks, bikes, pools, spas, and restaurants, are included in your stay. Some hotels may charge an additional fee for certain services, while others may provide them free or at a reduced rate.

6. Read reviews and look at images from prior guests: Reading reviews and looking at images of past guests is one of the greatest methods to get a sense of what to expect from your Bora Bora accommodation. You can utilize websites like [TripAdvisor] to get honest and detailed feedback from travelers who have stayed at the hotels you're considering. You can also examine images from other viewpoints and perspectives, such as the view from the bungalow, the size of the bathroom, the food quality, and the property's cleanliness. This can assist you in avoiding unpleasant surprises and making an educated decision.

Chapter 5

Things to Do

Water Activities

1. Aquabike Adventure: This is a one-of-a-kind and exciting way to explore Bora Bora's underwater world. You'll ride a two-seater submarine scooter that allows you to breathe normally underwater while appreciating the vibrant coral reefs and exotic wildlife. Swim with sharks and rays in a safe and regulated environment.

2. Kite Surf School Polynesie: If you want to learn how to kite surf, you can do so with experienced teachers. You'll learn the fundamentals of kite control, safety, and board riding before gliding over the waves and feeling the wind in your hair. You may also see the island and the lagoon from a different angle.

3. Reef Discovery Pure Snorkeling: This is the ideal activity for snorkeling fans, as you will visit four different locations around the island, each with its own distinct marine life. There will be anemone fish, moray eels, manta rays, eagle rays, and other creatures to observe. Along the walk, your guide will also tell you some legends and myths of Bora Bora.

4. Bora Bora Jet Ski Adventure: Ride a jet ski around the island with a local guide to discover Bora Bora's lagoon. You will stop at the volcano's crater, a beautiful swimming hole, and other stunning sites. Your guide will also teach you about Bora Bora's history and culture.

5. Bora Bora Luxury Tour and Beach Picnic: This is a calm and romantic activity in which you will sail around the lagoon on a cozy boat while being served appetizers and drinks. You'll also make a stop at a private motu (islet) for a delightful barbecue meal featuring fresh fish and local favorites. There will be time for swimming, snorkeling, or simply relaxing on the white sand beach.

Land Excursions

Here are five excursions that will take you to the island's hidden beauties if you want to discover the landside of Bora Bora.

1. 4x4 Safari Tour: This is one of Bora Bora's most popular and exciting land excursions. You will travel in a four-wheel-drive vehicle capable of handling the rocky and steep roads leading to the island's interior. You will see rich tropical foliage, old archaeological sites, World War II guns, and stunning vistas of the lagoon and adjacent islands along the way. Your local guide will also educate you on the history, culture, and tales of Bora Bora. This excursion is offered by several firms, including Tupuna Mountain Safari, Maohi Nui Tours, Vavau Adventures, and Bora Bora Safari Land.

2. Circle Island Road journey: For a more relaxed and gorgeous land trip, enjoy a journey on the island's only paved road, the Circle Island Road. It's roughly 32 kilometers long and takes you along the coast, past white sand beaches, coconut farms, charming communities, and historical sites. This tour can be taken by bus, bike, scooter, or even on foot. The Matira Beach, Bloody Mary's Restaurant, Faanui Bay, and the Marae Aehautai (a sacred location where ancient ceremonies were held) are among the highlights of this excursion.

3. Hiking Tour: Hiking is a terrific method for more adventurous and fit people to see the natural beauty and fauna of Bora Bora. There are numerous trails to choose from, ranging from easy to difficult. Some of the most popular are the Mount Otemanu Trail, which leads to the base of the island's iconic peak; the Mount Pahia Trail, which leads to the island's second highest point; and the Valley of the Kings Trail, which leads to a hidden waterfall through a lush forest. You can trek on your own or participate in a guided tour led by a local expert, such as Bora Bora Hiking or Bora Bora Explorer.

4. Horseback Riding Tour: Exploring the land side of Bora Bora by horseback is another fun and romantic option. You may enjoy the sights and breeze while riding down the beach, through the coconut plantations, or up the hills. Along the route, you can stop for a picnic or a swim. Bora Bora Ranch, Bora Bora Horseback Riding, and Bora Bora Equestrian Center are among the horseback riding tours available on the island.

5. Cultural Tour: If you wish to discover more about Bora Bora's rich and diverse culture, you can join a cultural tour that will introduce you to the Polynesian people's traditions, customs, arts, and crafts. Visit a local town, witness a dance performance, learn how to make flower crowns or pareos, sample local cuisine, or even take part in a fire-walking ceremony. Bora Bora Cultural Island Day Tour, Bora Bora Polynesian Cultural Experience, and Bora Bora Cultural Lagoon Tour are among the cultural trips available.

Cultural Experiences

Here are the cultural activities available in Bora Bora:

1. Tahitian Ahi Ma'a: This is a traditional Tahitian method of cooking food in an underground oven with firewood, lava rocks, and banana leaves. Wrapped in leaves, the meal is buried in the pit for many hours, resulting in a delicate and smokey dish. You can enjoy this dish at one of the local restaurants or hotels, or you can join a cultural trip that includes a cooking demonstration.

2. Art Galleries and Studios: Bora Bora is home to many brilliant artists who create paintings, sculptures, carvings, and jewelry inspired by the natural beauty and culture of the island. You can go to the studios of well-known artists like Alain Despert and Gilles Ossa, or you can peruse the art galleries and shops that sell local artwork. You can also buy souvenirs or gifts that highlight Bora Bora's artistic flair.

3. Bora Bora Tamure: This is a style of dance that features rhythmic hip motions accompanied by drums, ukuleles, and singing. The dancers are dressed in brightly colored outfits made of flowers, shells, and feathers. The tenure is a form of expression for joy, love, and appreciation, as well as a means of conveying stories and legends. Some hotels and resorts provide more shows, or you can join a cultural tour that includes a dancing class.

4. Musée De La Marine: A tiny museum displaying models of ships and boats that have traveled in the Pacific Ocean, ranging from ancient Polynesian canoes to modern yachts. In addition, the museum displays historical images and papers that illustrate the tale of Bora Bora's maritime past, particularly its position as a military base during World War II.

5. Local Festivals: Throughout the year, Bora Bora celebrates several festivals that highlight its culture and customs. **Among the most well-known are:**

- **Heiva:** A month-long celebration in July that includes competitions in sports, music, dancing, and crafts. It is a time to commemorate ancestors, gods, and the land while also having fun and socializing.

- **Tiurai:** This celebration, held on July 14, commemorates the French influence on Bora Bora. Parades, fireworks, and cultural events are all part of it.

- **Matari'i i ni'a:** In November, the Pleiades star cluster rises in the sky, signaling the beginning of the summer season. It is a time to honor nature's bounty and the fertility of the land via ceremonies, offerings, and feasts.

Chapter 6

Dining and Cuisine

Local Delicacies

Bora Bora is a lovely French Polynesian island with wonderful cuisine. **Here are ten Bora Bora specialties that you can eat or prepare at home.**

1. Poisson cru (raw fish): This is the national dish of French Polynesia. Fresh tuna marinated in lime juice and coconut milk is blended with sliced cucumber, tomato, and onion. It's frequently accompanied by rice or breadfruit.

2. Mahi Mahi in coconut milk: A famous fish meal cooked with coconut milk, ginger, and other local spices. Mahi Mahi is a solid and moist-textured dolphin fish.

The coconut milk lends a creamy, rich flavor to the dish, which is typically eaten with breadfruit or taro root.

3. Sushi: Sushi is a Japanese cuisine that has been tailored to Bora Bora's native ingredients and flavors. It's created using fresh fish like tuna, salmon, or octopus, as well as vinegar and sugar-seasoned sweet rice. Sushi is frequently wrapped in seaweed and garnished with sesame seeds, avocado, or mango.

4. Foie gras: Foie gras is a French delicacy produced from the fattened liver of a duck or goose. Foie gras is made with indigenous eggplant, spices, and honey in Bora Bora. Seared foie gras is served with a sweet and tangy sauce.

5. Rotisserie pork: Rotisserie pig is juicy and supple meat that is roasted over an open fire on a spit. The pork is seasoned with salt, pepper, garlic, and herbs before being basted in its juices. The grilled pineapple segments provide a tropical and refreshing touch to the pork.

6. Tahitian vanilla panna cotta: Tahitian vanilla is an island-grown vanilla with a distinct aroma and flavor. Panna cotta is a traditional Italian dessert comprised of cream, sugar, and gelatin. Tahitian vanilla flavors the panna cotta, which is refrigerated until set. It's generally accompanied by fresh fruits like berries, kiwi, or passion fruit.

7. Banana or papaya puree: This is a quick and easy dessert made with mashed bananas or papayas and flavored with vanilla, honey, or coconut milk. The purée is cooked till brown and bubbling before serving warm or cold. It has the consistency of pudding and a fruity flavor.

8. ka mata: Ika mata is a dish similar to poisson cru, however, it is prepared differently. It is made using raw fish, such as snapper, that has been marinated in lime juice and coconut cream and is tossed with chopped vegetables including carrot, cabbage, and onion. It's served chilled and seasoned with salt, pepper, and cilantro.

9. Rosh bora: Rosh bora is a sweet and delicious snack cooked from soaked, ground, and fried urad dal, a type of lentil. After that, the fritters are steeped in sugar syrup and dusted with coconut flakes. On the inside, they're soft and fluffy, while on the exterior, they're crispy and sticky.

10. Bora berry tart: Bora berry is an island-native berry with a sweet and sour flavor. It is used to make a delectable tart with coconut flour and sugarcane jaggery crust, bora berry jam, fresh bora berries, and whipped cream on top. It's a light and luscious summer dessert.

Popular Restaurants

Here are six prominent Bora Bora eateries that you should not miss on your trip.

Jean-Georges' Lagoon

The St. Regis Bora Bora Resort's Lagoon Restaurant by Jean-Georges is one of the island's most recognized restaurants. The restaurant is situated above the sea and provides breathtaking views of the lagoon and Mount Otemanu. The renowned chef Jean-Georges Vongerichten devised the menu, which comprises contemporary and fusion meals made with local products and fresh fish. The tuna is presented in four ways, the black pearl chocolate dessert, and the lobster and coconut milk soup are among the signature dishes. The restaurant also boasts French Polynesia's largest wine vault, with over 2,000 wines to pick from. The Lagoon Restaurant by Jean-Georges is only open for dinner, and reservations are strongly advised.

La Villa Mahana

La Estate Mahana is a lovely estate near Matira Beach that has a cozy and intimate restaurant. Chef Damien Rinaldi-Dovio oversees the restaurant, which provides a personalized and exquisite dining experience. The menu changes every day depending on ingredients and the chef's ideas, but it always includes French, Mediterranean, and Polynesian flavors. The foie gras with mango chutney, lamb chops with rosemary sauce, and vanilla crème brûlée are just a few of the meals available. The chef has also meticulously picked a wine list of over 100 bottles for the restaurant. La Villa Mahana features only seven tables, making it incredibly private and romantic. To reserve a space, you must book well in advance.

Bora Bora Yacht Club

Bora Bora Yacht Club is a laid-back waterfront restaurant near Vaitape. Since 1972, the restaurant has served locals and guests, and it is a popular hangout for boaters, sailors, and yachters. The menu includes everything from burgers and pizzas to salads and sandwiches, but the seafood, particularly the fish and chips, mahi-mahi burger, and tuna steak, is the house specialty. There's also a bar where you may sip a martini, a beer, or a glass of wine while viewing the sunset or the stars. Bora Bora Yacht Club is open for lunch and supper, and on some nights, it also organizes live music and activities.

Bloody Marys

Bloody Mary's is a legendary Bora Bora restaurant known for its rustic decor, celebrity clientele, and the cocktail of the same name. The restaurant is made of natural materials like bamboo, palm leaves, and sand, and it has an unusual feature: you must remove your shoes and walk barefoot on the floor. The menu is based on the catch of the day, which can be selected from an ice display. You can also choose how your fish is cooked, as well as the sauces and sides you prefer. Grilled tuna, poisson cru, lobster, and shrimp are some of the alternatives. In addition to meat, chicken, and vegetarian entrees, the restaurant also serves sweets and beverages. Bloody Mary's serves lunch and dinner and includes a gift shop and shuttle service.

Bora Bora Beach Club and Restaurant

Bora Bora Beach Club and Restaurant is a laid-back and enjoyable restaurant located on Matira Beach. The restaurant includes a beachside terrace where you can enjoy the breeze and a view of the lagoon. The menu includes everything from pizzas and pasta to burgers and wraps, but the centerpiece is Polynesian food, which includes dishes like coconut chicken, fish curry, and fish cru. There is also a bar where you can order a cocktail, a smoothie, or juice while listening to live music or watching sports on television. Bora Bora Beach Club and Restaurant serves breakfast, lunch, and dinner daily and rents out loungers, umbrellas, and kayaks.

Le Corail

The InterContinental Bora Bora Resort & Thalasso Spa's Le Corail restaurant is refined and exquisite. The restaurant is Bora Bora's sole fine dining establishment that serves a degustation menu of 5 or 7 dishes matched with wines. The menu changes seasonally, but it always highlights the chef's ingenuity and ability by utilizing high-quality ingredients and novel techniques. You can come across meals like foie gras with passion fruit, scallops with truffle, and a chocolate sphere with caramel. The restaurant also has French Polynesia's largest wine vault, with over 2,000 wines to pick from. Reservations are necessary for dinner at Le Corail.

Tip For Booking Ahead

Here are recommendations for reserving restaurants in Bora Bora.

1. Plan ahead of time and book online

The first and most crucial suggestion is to plan ahead of time and book online. Some of the restaurants in Bora Bora, such as Lagoon Restaurant by Jean-Georges, La Villa Mahana, and Le Corail, are quite exclusive and have limited seating capacity. They demand reservations months in advance, sometimes even years in advance. You can book online through their websites or your hotel's concierge. Booking online also allows you to verify the restaurants' availability, menu, rates, and dress code.

2. Consider the location and transit options.

The second advice is to think about the restaurants' location and transportation options. Bora Bora is a small island that is separated into multiple motus (islets) and a main island. Some of the restaurants are on the main island, such as Bora Bora Yacht Club and Bloody

Mary's, while others are on motus, such as Lagoon Restaurant by Jean-Georges, Le Corail, and Bora Bora Beach Club and Restaurant. Depending on where you are staying, you may need to take a boat, a car, or a bike to get to the eateries. Before booking, you should examine the distance and transit choices and plan accordingly. Some restaurants, such as Bloody Mary's, provide a free shuttle service from your hotel, while others, such as Lagoon Restaurant by Jean-Georges and Le Corail, require a price for the boat transfer.

3. Be open to new possibilities.

The third piece of advice is to be adaptable and try new things. Bora Bora boasts a wide range of restaurants, from fine dining to informal, from French to Polynesian, from fish to steak. Bora Bora has something to fit everyone's taste and budget, although you may need to be flexible and try different possibilities. If you can't obtain a reservation at Jean-Georges' Lagoon Restaurant, for example, try Le Corail, which also has a degustation menu and a wine cellar. If you can't obtain a table at La Villa Mahana, consider Bora Bora Beach Club and

Restaurant, which also serves Polynesian food and has a beachfront patio. If Bloody Mary's is full, consider Bora Bora Yacht Club, which offers a rustic setting and a seafood menu.

4. Examine the reviews and ratings

The fourth suggestion is to read the restaurant reviews and ratings before making a reservation. Bora Bora has several restaurants, however, not all of them are equally wonderful. On websites like TripAdvisor, Yelp, and Google, you can obtain honest and helpful feedback from other tourists who have visited the eateries. On these websites, you may also view restaurant ratings, images, prices, and menus. This will assist you in selecting the best restaurants for your interests and expectations.

5. Take in the local delicacies and atmosphere.

The fifth and last recommendation is to enjoy the local dishes as well as the environment of the restaurants. Bora Bora has a rich and diversified culinary culture influenced by French, Polynesian, Asian, and international cuisines. There are meals such as poisson cru (raw fish marinated in lime juice and coconut milk), mahi-mahi (a type of fish), foie gras (duck or goose liver), and vanilla (an island spice). You can also enjoy the ambiance of the restaurants, which might be romantic, rustic, classy, or exciting. You can dine on the sea, on the beach, in a home, or at a yacht club. You can also eat while watching the sunset, the stars, or the fire dancers. Bora Bora has something for everyone, so enjoy every minute and bite.

Nightlife and Bars

If you want to have some fun and entertainment when the sun goes down, **here are five nightlife activities and clubs in Bora Bora to try.**

1. La Cave - Bora Bora: A wine bar with a warm and intimate ambiance, as well as a collection of wines from across the world, cheese, charcuterie, and tapas. You can also purchase bottles of wine to take home or drink in your hotel room. La Cave is located in Vaitape, Bora

Bora's main hamlet, and is accessible Monday through Saturday from 5 p.m. to 10 p.m.

2. Bubble Bar: A sleek and modern bar located poolside at the St. Regis Resort, with views of the beach and the lagoon. You can drink cocktails, wine, champagne, or beer while nibbling on nibbles or light meals from the menu. On some nights, the bar also includes live music and DJ sets, as well as a giant screen for sports events. Bubble Bar is open from 10 a.m. to 11 p.m. daily.

3. Sunset Bar: Another bar in the Four Seasons Resort with a beautiful view of the lagoon and Mount Otemanu, Bora Bora's renowned peak. You can enjoy a drink or a meal from the menu, which includes sushi, burgers, salads, and desserts while watching the sunset. There is also a happy hour from 5 to 6 p.m. with live music on some nights. Sunset Bar is open from 4 p.m. to 11 p.m. daily.

4. Sunset trip: If you want to see the lagoon and the sky at nightfall, you can book a sunset catamaran trip. You will be picked up from your hotel pier and brought to the opposite side of the island to see the hues of the sunset and stars. You'll also get a free beverage, with or without alcohol, and some appetizers. The cruise lasts around two hours and is offered on Mondays, Wednesdays, and Fridays.

5. Matira Beach: With a long stretch of white sand and clear sea, this is Bora Bora's most popular and accessible beach. Relax on the beach, swim, snorkel, or kayak, and gaze out over the lagoon and mountains. There are also various bars and restaurants along the beach where you can enjoy a drink or a snack while watching the moonlight on the water. Matira Beach is open to the public and free to visit.

Chapter 7

Shopping in Bora Bora

Popular Shopping Areas

Here are five must-see retail spots in Bora Bora:

1. Alain Despert's Studio and Gallery: This is the studio and gallery of Alain Despert, a well-known French painter who has lived in Bora Bora since 1986. His passionate and vivid paintings convey the essence of the island and its culture. You can view his original artwork, prints, and posters at his studio by appointment. Some of his designs can also be purchased as souvenirs or gifts.

2. Sibani Perles: This is the place to go for genuine Tahitian pearls. For almost 30 years, Sibani Perles has been creating and selling high-quality pearls. You can select from a variety of pearl jewelry, ranging from basic earrings to beautiful necklaces, or you can make your own. The team is experienced and polite, and they will assist you in finding the ideal pearl for you.

3. Arc En Ciel Bora-Bora: This beautiful gift shop carries a range of local handicrafts, including pareos, sarongs, purses, caps, and accessories. Handmade items, including wood carvings, coconut shells, and shell jewelry, are also available. Melanie, who runs the shop, is friendly and helpful. She can also help you plan island tours and activities.

4. Bora Art Upstairs: A quiet art gallery showcasing the works of local artists such as paintings, sculptures, and photography. You can explore the various styles and subjects to discover the talent and diversity of Bora Bora's art scene. Isabelle owns the gallery and is an avid art collector. She can teach you more about the artists and their backgrounds, as well as assist you in finding the ideal item for your home or business.

5. Tahia Exquisite Tahitian Pearls -Bora Bora: This is another pearl boutique with a beautiful range of Tahitian pearl jewelry, from classic to contemporary styles. The beauty and quality of the pearls, which come in a variety of forms, sizes, and colors, can be appreciated. You can also learn more about pearl farming, grading, and pearl maintenance. The personnel are pleasant and professional, and they will help you with your purchases.

Souvenirs and Gifts

Here are ten ideas for souvenirs and gifts to bring back from your trip:

1. Tahitian pearls: Bora Bora is well-known for its cultured black pearls, which are available in a variety of forms, sizes, hues, and quality. Many jewelry stores on the island carry them, including [Arc En Ciel Bora-Bora], [Sibani Perles], [Tahia Exquisite Tahitian Pearls], [Baldini Perles], and others. Pearls are a classic and elegant present that can be worn for any occasion and in any manner.

2. Monoi oil: A traditional Tahitian product created from coconut oil and tiare flowers, monoi oil is a fragrant, emollient oil. It has a light flowery scent and can be used to moisturize the skin, hair, and nails. Monoi oil is available in a variety of forms, including soap, shampoo, lotion, perfume, and candles. Monoi oil is available at [Albert Store], [Boutique Bora Bora], and [L'Atelier Nuanua].

3. Vanilla: Vanilla is another popular commodity from French Polynesia due to the islands' great growing conditions for vanilla orchids. Vanilla beans, pods, and extracts are used to flavor sweets, drinks, and other foods. Vanilla items can be purchased at [Albert Store], [Bora Bora Original], and [Jena Jewelry Bora Bora].

4. Pareo: Pareo is a vibrant and adaptable fabric that can be worn as a wrap, skirt, dress, scarf, or sarong. It is a popular piece of apparel in Bora Bora and other Polynesian islands, and it is available in a variety of patterns, colors, and materials. Many souvenir shops, such as [Bora Bora Original], [Boutique Bora Bora], and [Tresors by Tahia], sell pareos.

5. Tiki: A carved wooden or stone representation of Polynesia's primordial gods. They are frequently seen as protective, powerful, and fertile symbols. Tiki statues, masks, and pendants can be found in a variety of souvenir shops, including [Bora Bora Original], [Boutique Bora Bora], and [Tahiti Pearl Market].

6. Shell jewelry: Because the island is rich in marine life and shells, shell jewelry is another popular souvenir from Bora Bora. Cowries, conches, clams, and oysters are used to create necklaces, bracelets, earrings, and rings. Shell jewelry can be purchased at [La Perle de MAIMITI], [Robert Wan Bora Bora Boutiques], and [Tahiti Pearl Market] among other places.

7. Coconut products: A staple food and resource in Bora Bora and other Polynesian islands, coconut is a staple food and resource. Coconut is used to make a variety of goods, including coconut water, milk, cream, oil, sugar, and flakes. Coconut crafts such as bowls, cups, spoons, and baskets are also available. Coconut items can be purchased at the [Albert Store], [Bora Bora Original], and [L'Atelier Nuanua].

8. Art: Because of its Polynesian background and French colonization, Bora Bora has a rich and diverse artistic tradition. There are paintings, sculptures, carvings, pottery, and textiles depicting the scenery, fauna, and inhabitants of the island. [Bora Bora Original], [L'Atelier Nuanua], and [Tahiti Pearl Market] are some venues where you may buy artwork.

9. Coffee: Another crop that thrives in the tropical climate of Bora Bora and other Polynesian islands is coffee. Coffee beans, grounds, and pods with a rich, smooth flavor and aroma are available. There are various coffee accessories available, such as mugs, cups, and filters. Coffee is available in [Albert Store], [Bora Bora Original], and [Tahiti Pearl Market].

10. Chocolate: Chocolate is a delectable and decadent dessert that everybody can enjoy. Chocolate bars, truffles, pralines, and bonbons created with local ingredients including vanilla, coconut, pineapple, and banana are available. There are other chocolate presents available, such as boxes, baskets, and bouquets. Chocolate is available at [Albert Store], [Bora Bora Original], and [Tahiti Pearl Market].

Chapter 8

Practical Tips

Safety Tips and Health Precautions

As with any trip destination, there are some safety measures and health considerations to be aware of before you arrive. **Here are a few of the most significant:**

1. Crime: Bora Bora has a low crime rate and is generally regarded as a safe destination for tourists. Take care of your valuables, however, and avoid leaving them unattended or in plain sight. Pickpockets and scammers should also be avoided in congested areas, such as Vaitape's main port1. If you have any problems, call 17 or the gendarmerie at 40 67 72 00.

2. Sun: Bora Bora has a tropical environment with plenty of sunshine all year. Sunburn, heatstroke, and dehydration can all be avoided by constantly applying sunscreen, wearing a hat and sunglasses, drinking lots of water, and avoiding excessive alcohol use. Seek shade during the hottest hours of the day, which are normally between 10 a.m. and 2 p.m.

3. Water: The lagoon of Bora Bora is a lovely and appealing spot to swim, snorkel, and dive. Sharks, stingrays, barracudas, stonefish, urchins, and coral are all possible risks in the sea. Swimming at night, near river mouths, or in murky water should be avoided because these are more likely to attract sharks. You should also avoid touching or treading on any sea creatures or plants, as they could be venomous or cause diseases. When you are in the water, you should wear dependable foot protection, such as water shoes or reef shoes. If you wish to scuba dive, make sure you follow all safety precautions and avoid diving within 24 hours after landing.

4. Mosquitoes: Dengue fever, chikungunya, and the Zika virus are all spread by mosquitos in Bora Bora. Wear long-sleeved clothing, apply insect repellent, and sleep behind a mosquito net or in an air-conditioned environment to avoid mosquito bites. Before your travel, you should also check with your doctor to confirm that you have all of the essential immunizations and prescriptions.

5. Natural calamities: Natural disasters like hurricanes, tsunamis, earthquakes, and volcanic eruptions are common in Bora Bora. In the event of an emergency, you should keep an eye on the local weather and news broadcasts and obey the directions of the authorities. Additionally, you should register with your embassy or consulate and have travel insurance that covers medical bills and evacuation fees.

Bora Bora is a great and safe destination to visit as long as you follow some basic measures and respect nature and culture. You can enjoy your trip to Bora Bora and make wonderful memories if you follow these safety advice and health measures.

Local Customs and Etiquette

Before visiting Bora Bora, it is vital to learn about the island's customs and manners. **Here are pointers on how to respect and enjoy Bora Bora culture:**

1. Greeting: The residents are extremely polite and welcoming, and will greet you with a warm "ia ora na" (hello) and a smile. Returning the greeting and shaking hands is considered polite. To express your gratitude and appreciation, you can also say "murmur" (thank you).

2. Dressing: Bora Bora is a laid-back location, but while visiting native villages or religious sites, you should dress modestly. When leaving the pool or beach area, cover up your swimsuits and put on boots. Wearing revealing or tight attire that could be perceived as insulting or disrespectful should be avoided.

3. Dining: Because much of the food in Bora Bora is imported from other countries, it is highly pricey. As a result, you should try the indigenous food, which consists primarily of fish, coconut, breadfruit, taro, and other fruits and vegetables. Tahitian ahi ma'a is a traditional cuisine that consists of meat, fish, and vegetables cooked in an underground oven. This culinary style can be tried at some resorts or local events. When dining out, pay the bill at the front of the restaurant rather than at the table, as is customary. You should also tip 10% of the whole amount, as this is expected and appreciated by the personnel.

4. Gift-giving: If you are welcomed to a local's home, you should bring a small gift to demonstrate your appreciation, such as flowers, chocolates, or wine. You should also commend the host on the quality of their home and meal, and offer to help with the dishes or cleaning. You should not refuse food or drink because it may be perceived as disrespectful or ungrateful.

5. Photography: Bora Bora is a photogenic island, and you'll want to capture the beauty and memories of your visit. However, as a measure of respect and civility, you should always ask permission before photographing residents, particularly youngsters. You should also refrain from photographing sacred or cultural places like temples, marae (old stone platforms), or petroglyphs (rock engravings) unless you receive permission from the authorities or people.

6. Environment: Bora Bora is a delicate and valuable ecosystem that should be protected and preserved. Natural or cultural resources such as coral, shells, plants, or artifacts should not be littered, damaged, or removed. You should also avoid feeding, touching, or bothering wildlife and aquatic life. You should abide by the norms and regulations of the national park, marine reserve, and resorts, and use environmentally friendly products and practices whenever feasible.

Packing Essentials

Bora Bora is many tourists' dream vacation, but packing for this tropical paradise can be difficult. You want to be prepared for the sun, sea, and adventure, but you also don't want to overpack and incur additional fees. **Here are some must-pack goods for Bora Bora to help you prepare for your trip.**

Sunscreen and sun-care products

Bora Bora's heat can be scorching, especially if you're not acclimated to it. If you don't want a terrible sunburn to mar your vacation, bring plenty of sunscreen with a high SPF and broad-spectrum protection. After a day in the sun, pack some after-sun care items, such as aloe vera gel or lotion, to soothe and nourish your skin.

A rash guard and water shoes are required.

Bora Bora is well-known for its crystal-clear lagoon, where you can go snorkeling, swimming, kayaking, and other water sports. Wear a rash guard and water shoes in the ocean to protect yourself from the heat, coral, and marine life. A rash guard is a long-sleeved, quick-drying clothing that covers your entire chest and arms. Water shoes are shoes with a rubber sole and a mesh upper that are intended to be worn in water. They'll keep you from stumbling over jagged rocks, coral, or sea urchins.

Snorkeling equipment with an underwater camera

The incredible marine life that inhabits the lagoon is one of Bora Bora's features. You may witness a variety of colorful fish, rays, sharks, turtles, and other marine life. Bring your snorkeling equipment and underwater camera to truly experience this underwater beauty. A snorkel, a mask, and fins are the components of snorkeling equipment. You can rent them from your resort or tour operator, but they might not fit you correctly or be adequately cleaned. You will be more comfortable and safe if you bring your own. You'll be able to capture the beauty of the lagoon with an underwater camera and share it with your friends and family. You can use a smartphone waterproof case, a GoPro, or an underwater camera.

Cover-ups and swimwear

You'll probably spend most of your time in Bora Bora wearing swimwear, so bring at least three or four outfits. You can mix and match tops and bottoms, or go for one-piece swimsuits. Bring some cover-ups, such as sun dresses, sarongs, or kimonos, to wear over your swimsuit while walking around the resort, going to lunch, or exploring the island. Cover-ups will keep you warm in the sun and show respect for the local culture.

Rope and floats

You will have immediate access to the lagoon from your deck if you stay in an overwater bungalow. Bringing some inflatable floaties and a rope is a fun way to relax and enjoy the scenery. The floaties can be inflated with a pump or by mouth, and they can be tied to your deck with a rope. Then you may relax in the water on the floaties without fear of drifting away. Floaties come in a variety of shapes and sizes, such as flamingos, donuts, and unicorns.

Clothing and jacket that are light in weight

Bora Bora has a tropical climate with year-round temperatures ranging from 25°C to 30°C (79°F to 82°F). Pack cotton t-shirts, shorts, skirts, and outfits that are light and breathable. You should also pack a light jacket or sweater in case it gets cold at night or rains. Bora Bora is prone to rain showers, especially between November and April, so bring a rain jacket or an umbrella.

Beach towel and hat

A beach bag is a must-have item for Bora Bora because you will need to carry your belongings with you when you visit the beach, lagoon, or island. Look for a beach bag that is roomy, long-lasting, and water-resistant. It should include several pockets and compartments to keep your belongings organized, such as sunscreen, a towel, a water bottle, a camera, and a wallet. Pack a hat to protect your face and eyes from the sun. A hat that can being readily folded or scrunched up and will not blow off in the wind is great.

Visas and passports

Bora Bora is located in French Polynesia, which is a French overseas possession. To enter the country, you must have a valid passport, and, depending on your nationality, you may also need a visa. Before you go, you should research the visa requirements as well as the entry and exit criteria for your location. In case of loss or theft, you should also create duplicates of your passport and visa and store them separately from the originals.

Mozzie repellant and itching cream

Mosquitoes can be a bother in Bora Bora, especially during the rainy season, which lasts from November to April. To avoid and treat insect bites, bring mosquito repellent and anti-itch cream. Look for a repellent that contains DEET, picaridin, or lemon eucalyptus oil, and apply it to exposed skin regularly. Wear long sleeves and pants, and avoid standing water, where mosquitoes grow.

If you are bitten, use anti-itch cream on the affected region and avoid scratching to avoid infection and scars.

Converters and adapters

Bora Bora's electrical system is the same as that of France, which is 220 volts and 50 hertz. Type C and E plugs and sockets have two round pins. To utilize your electrical gadgets if you are traveling from a nation that uses a different voltage, frequency, or plug type, you will need an adapter and a converter. A gadget that allows you to plug your device into a different type of socket is known as an adapter. A converter is a device that alters the voltage and frequency of electricity to match the needs of your equipment. Check the labels on your devices to determine if they are compatible with your destination's electrical system and if not, pack the proper adaptor and converter. You should also avoid overloading the sockets, which might result in damage or fire.

These are the most crucial goods to bring to Bora Bora, but you should also bring sunglasses, flip-flops, sandals, toiletries, prescriptions, novels, and games. Check the dress code of your resort as well as the restaurants you intend to visit, as some may need more formal clothes for dinner or special occasions. Make sure to leave room in your suitcase for mementos and memories from this incredible island.

Emergency Contacts

As with any other vacation, it is critical to be prepared for any emergency scenarios that may happen during your visit. **Here are helpful hints and contacts for Bora Bora visitors:**

1. Emergency numbers: Dial 17 from any landline or mobile phone in the event of a medical, fire, or police emergency. This is the equivalent of dialing 911 in the United States or 112 in Europe. You can also dial 15 for an ambulance or 18 for the fire department.

2. Medical center: A medical center is located in the main town of Vaitape on Bora Bora. It provides basic health care services such as consultations, medications, immunizations, and minor operations. Monday through Friday, 7:30 a.m. to 4:30 p.m., and Saturday, 7:30 a.m. to 11:30 a.m. The phone number is 40 67 60 00.

3. Hospital: While medical care for significant difficulties is not available in Bora Bora, the hospital facilities in Papeete, Tahiti's capital, are superb. In an emergency, medical evacuation services using local airlines, military planes, or helicopters will airlift you to the general hospital in Papeete. The hospital offers a 24-hour emergency room, a decompression chamber for divers, and specialists in a variety of specialties. The phone number is 40 48 81 81.

4. Pharmacy: There is one pharmacy on Bora Bora, which is likewise located in Vaitape. It is open Monday through Friday from 7:30 a.m. to 5:00 p.m., and Saturday from 7:30 a.m. to 12:00 p.m. The phone number is 40 67 60 60.

5. Dentist: There is just one dentist in Bora Bora, and he works at the medical facility. The phone number is 40 67 60 00.

6. Consulates: There is no foreign embassy in French Polynesia, although approximately 20 nations maintain honorary consulate officers who can assist passengers in the event of a problem. For example, the United States has a consular agency in Papeete with the phone number 40 42 65 35. The list of other consulates can be found on the French High Commission's official website.

7. Travel insurance: It is strongly advised to purchase travel insurance that covers medical expenditures, evacuation, repatriation, and cancellation. You can compare and buy travel insurance online from a variety of companies, including World Nomads, Allianz Travel, and AXA Assistance.

Chapter 9

Itineraries

One Day Itinerary

Snorkeling and a Lagoon Cruise in the Morning

Begin the day with a lagoon boat and snorkeling exploration of the island and its nearby motus (little islets). You'll get to observe the various marine species that live on coral reefs, such as colorful fish, rays, and sharks. Some excursions also include a stop at a pearl farm, where you can learn about the growth and harvesting of these valuable gems. A four-hour lagoon cruise and snorkeling tour normally includes hotel pickup and drop-off, snorkeling equipment, and refreshments.

4WD excursion and lunch at afternoon

After your aquatic excursion, rent a 4WD car and explore Bora Bora's inland. A 4WD tour will take you to some of the most beautiful places on the island, including the Matira overlook, ancient marae (holy sites), and World War II guns. You'll also get a good look at the lagoon and Mount Otemanu, the majestic peak that dominates the area. A four-wheel drive tour typically lasts three hours and includes hotel pickup and drop-off, a guide, and lunch at a nearby restaurant.

Evening activities include a sunset cruise and dinner.

Finish your day with a romantic sunset boat followed by dinner at one of the island's finest restaurants. A sunset cruise allows you to enjoy the beautiful colors of the sky as the sun sets below the horizon while sipping champagne and snacking. Along the way, you might even see some dolphins or whales. Following the cruise, you will be transferred to a restaurant of your choosing, where you will be able to enjoy a fantastic supper of local or foreign cuisine. A sunset cruise and dinner lasts around four hours and includes hotel pick-up and drop-off, a boat trip, champagne, appetizers, and dinner.

15 Days Itinerary

If you want to visit this tropical paradise, here is a sample 14-day itinerary to help you make the most of your time and money.

Day 1: Arrive in Tahiti and transfer to Moorea

Take a short flight or ferry from Tahiti to Moorea, Tahiti's sister island. Moorea is famous for its spectacular beauty, lush mountains, and blue lagoon. Check into your hotel and unwind for the remainder of the day. You can select from overwater bungalows, beachfront villas, or garden cottages.

Day 2: Beach day in Moorea

On Moorea, you can spend the day relaxing in the sun, sand, and sea. In the pristine sea, you can swim, snorkel, kayak, or paddleboard, or just relax on the beach with a nice book. You can also explore the island by bike, scooter, or car, stopping at sites like the Belvedere overlook, pineapple plantations, and the Moorea Tropical Garden.

Day 3: Moorea whale swimming or scuba diving

You may swim with humpback whales at Moorea if you visit between July and November. You may join a guided tour to view these gentle giants up close as they travel to the warm seas of French Polynesia to mate and give birth. If whales are not your thing, you can go scuba diving instead. Moorea features some of the world's top dive locations, with vivid coral reefs, abundant marine life, and even buried wrecks.

Day 4: Moore's Interior

Today, you will explore Moore's interior, which is just as beautiful as the coast. Explore the island's beautiful valleys, waterfalls, and archaeological sites by joining a guided trek, 4x4 safari, or horseback riding excursion. You'll also learn about the Polynesian people's culture and history, as well as sample some of their native delicacies.

Day 5: Beach day in Huahine

After breakfast, board a trip to Huahine, one of French Polynesia's most original and pristine islands. Huahine is made up of two islands: Huahine Nui (large) and Huahine Iti (little), which are linked by a bridge. Check into your hotel and relax on the beach for the rest of the day. Huahine boasts some of the region's most pristine and quiet beaches, where you can relax and take in the natural beauty.

Day 6: Tour of the Huahine Lagoon

Today, you'll go snorkeling in Huahine's lagoon, which is teeming with marine life and coral gardens. You can take a boat excursion to the greatest snorkeling areas and observe colorful fish, rays, sharks, and turtles. You will also go to a pearl farm to learn about the cultivation and harvesting of the famed black pearls. Lunch will be served on a motu, a small islet in the lagoon, and will include traditional Polynesian foods and music.

Day 7: Huahine cultural highlights

On your final day in Huahine, you will explore some of the island's cultural and historical sites. Huahine has the highest concentration of pre-European temples, known as marae, in French Polynesia. The precious blue-eyed eels, vanilla plantations, the sacred lake, and the Maeva village, where you can observe how the inhabitants live and work, are also on display.

Day 8: Arrive in Bora Bora

Fly to Bora Bora, French Polynesia's most famous and luxurious island. Bora Bora is famous for its unique overwater bungalows, Mount Otemanu, and the world's most picturesque lagoon. Check into your hotel and relax in your room with a view of the lagoon and the mountain.

Day 9: ATV tour of Bora Bora

On an ATV tour of Bora Bora today, you will have some fun and adventure. You will drive your own ATV, or share one with a companion, and will be led by a guide to the greatest sites on the island. The WWII cannons, the historic marae, the fruit farms, and the panoramic vistas will all be visible. You will also get time on your own to explore the island.

Day 10: Bora Bora beach paradise

Spend the day relaxing and exploring Bora Bora's beach and lagoon. In the crystal clear water, you can swim, snorkel, kayak, or paddleboard, or join a boat tour to observe the coral gardens and marine life. You can also attempt water sports like jet skiing, parasailing, and kite surfing. Alternatively, you can simply unwind on the beach or in your bungalow and indulge in a massage or spa treatment.

Day 11: Arrive in Rangiroa

Fly to Rangiroa, the largest atoll in French Polynesia and the world's second-largest. Rangiroa is a ring of coral islands encircling a large lagoon with some of the world's best diving and snorkeling. Check into your hotel and relax on the beach for the rest of the day. You can select between overwater bungalows, beachside bungalows, or guesthouses.

Day 12: Dolphin dive at Rangiroa

Today, you will have the once-in-a-lifetime opportunity to dive with dolphins in Rangiroa. You will board a dive boat that will transport you to Tiputa Pass, one of two passageways connecting the lagoon to the ocean. Hundreds of dolphins will play and interact with you. You'll also encounter sharks, rays, turtles, and fish. If you are not a diver, you can snorkel or take a dolphin-watching cruise instead.

Day 13: Tour of Rangiroa Blue Lagoon

Your final day in Rangiroa will include a visit to the Blue Lagoon, one of the most stunning and distinctive destinations in French Polynesia. A lagoon within a lagoon, the Blue Lagoon is a natural pool of turquoise water surrounded by coral islets and palm trees. You will take a boat tour to the Blue Lagoon, where you will be able to swim, snorkel, and relax on the beach. You will also see the Pink Sands, a beach with pink coral sand, and Bird Island, a seabird sanctuary.

Day 14: Arrive in Tahiti

Return to Tahiti, the major island of French Polynesia, by airplane. Tahiti is the region's cultural and economic capital, with a plethora of attractions, activities, and nightlife to offer. Check into your hotel and spend the remainder of the day relaxing in Tahiti. Visit the Papeete market, the Pearl Museum, the Gauguin Museum, or the Botanical Garden. Souvenirs such as pearls, vanilla, and handicrafts can also be purchased. Alternatively, you can partake in the nightlife, which includes pubs, restaurants, and clubs.

Day 15: Leave Tahiti

On your final day, you will bid French Polynesia farewell and board your trip home. You will return home with priceless memories and photographs of your incredible journey to Bora Bora and beyond. Mauruuru (thank you) and nana (goodbye!).

Conclusion

Bora Bora is more than a vacation spot. It's a reality. A romantic, adventure, and relaxation haven. A destination where you can discover the beauty and culture of French Polynesia while making memories to last a lifetime.

Bora Bora has something for everyone, whether you're planning a honeymoon, a family holiday, or a solo getaway. You can stay in a beautiful overwater house, snorkel with colorful fish and friendly sharks, walk to the top of a dormant volcano, or simply take in the breathtaking views of the turquoise lagoon and Mount Otemanu.

But Bora Bora is more than just a beautiful landscape. It's also about the individuals. The people are friendly and will share their culture, music, and cuisine with you. You can learn to construct a flower crown, do the time, and sample the poisson cru. You can also discover more about the history and culture of this wonderful island by visiting the religious sites, pearl farms, and art galleries.

Bora Bora will enchant your senses, move your heart, and inspire your soul. It's a destination you'll never forget and want to visit again and again. It is a destination that should be on your bucket list, and you will be glad you went.

Thank you for selecting this book as your Bora Bora guide. I hope you had as much fun reading it as I did writing it. I hope that was useful, instructive, and entertaining to you. Most importantly, I hope you have a fantastic time in Bora Bora. Best wishes.